WOMEN
LIKE ME

Community

Sharing What We Know To Be True

COMPILED BY JULIE FAIRHURST
Copyright 2022
Julie Fairhurst – Rock Star Publishing
ISBN Paperback Edition: 978-1-990639-03-6
Cover Design and Interior Design by STOKE Publishing

www.womenlikemestories.com

WOMEN LIKE ME COMMUNITY

SHARING WHAT WE KNOW TO BE TRUE

JULIE FAIRHURST

ROCK STAR PUBLISHING

CONTENTS

PART 2

LEARN MORE ABOUT WOMEN LIKE ME

...

Nanette Mathews

"We all serve as a vessel to be messengers for one another.
Are you sharing the messages you are inspired to speak?
Someone is waiting to hear your words."

DO YOU LISTEN TO YOUR DREAMS?

In 2016, I was searching for my purpose and struggling to continue the pace of my successful real estate career that has spanned over 30 years. I loved my job and the over 2,500 clients I'd helped over the years. However, I lost my way and knew it was time for more. But what?

One night as I slept in the middle of the night, I experienced a profound life-changing dream. I was being led back from wherever I was, and I remember saying, I don't want to go back; I want to stay here with you; I was told.

No, you must go back. You are not finished yet.

I felt so confused and sad as I wanted to stay wherever I was at that moment. But I don't know my purpose; I cried out. I was then told; You, you are your purpose.

I remember feeling anxious and saying, I don't know what to do.

I was told one word, Write!

Welcome to Women Like Me

Julie Fairhurst

...

Steve Maraboli

"The truth is unless you let go unless you forgive yourself, unless you forgive the situation unless you realize that the situation is over, you cannot move forward."

INTRODUCTION

What do you know to be true? Have you contemplated this question in your life and within your belief system? Many of us haven't given it a second thought. However, it is one question you must ask yourself. What do you know to be true?

The women of our Women Like Me Community Group – Julie Fairhurst, have asked themselves this question and shared their answers. As you read each woman's words, you'll find that none of them are precisely the same. Each one wrote what they know to be true, and their answers are vastly different.

Depending on your upbringing, your current mindset, your belief system, how you see the world, and many other factors, what is true for you may not be true for another. And that is entirely okay. Our truths should be our own, and what is true for one person may not in any way be true for another.

We live different lives; therefore, we will all have different truths.

This question of what you know to be true, for some, can be a difficult question to answer. It involves sitting with yourself and contemplating your life and life's circumstances. The question requires the writer to go inward and look at their life. If you have never answered this question yourself, give it a try. You may find the words you write enlightening.

One thing I know to be true is that nothing ever stays the same. Life is constantly changing, and that is encouraging. If you're going through a tough time in your life, this truth would be a comfort to you. Similar to the saying, "all things shall pass, and this will too."

Another truth for me is that life is not fair. Someone will always have more, and someone will always have less. Others will be healthy, and some with be sick. There will always be someone doing better than me and someone doing worse off. For me, this truth helps me to be satisfied with my life from moment to moment.

Here are a few questions that might help you search for what you know to be true.

- What are you most grateful for?
- What is your favorite thing to do?
- What have you learned in your life so far?
- What is most important to you?
- What could you not give up in your life?

Sitting with yourself and pondering these questions about yourself and your life may help open a window to what you know to be true.

Another great exercise is to sit and write out everything you know is true. Then looking at your list, you may be able to delete some of your answers after giving them more thought.

Whatever will work for you, discovering what you know to be true is a fantastic way to dig deeper into who you are and what your passion may be. Possibly while reading the words of these incredible women who have written what they know to be true, their truth may get your mindset flowing, helping you understand your truth.

I have not yet mentioned that the proceeds for this book and all the community books go to charity. Our present charity is for breast cancer research.

Thank you for supporting our community and our charity. You have helped with your purchase.

With Gratitude,

Julie Fairhurst

Kalu Ndukwe Kalu

"The things you do for yourself are gone when you are gone,
but the things you do for others remain as your legacy."

PART 1

SHARING WHAT WE KNOW TO BE TRUE

1

CLAIRE NEILSEN
LOSING AND FINDING OURSELVES

This is dedicated to women, particularly mothers who have devoted their lives to others and have lost touch with themselves in the process. It is so important to have understanding and empathy for the mothers in our lives: ourselves, our own mothers, and all mothers in humanity. Many mothers take their job of parenting so seriously that in the process of taking care of everyone else, they forget about themselves. These are the women for which I have the greatest compassion and honor their commitment and sacrifice.

"She let herself go, and now she is old and bitter. "I have heard this statement more times than I can count, and it wasn't until I became middle-aged that I understood how unfair a judgment it is. Does anyone ever stop to think about the story behind "Letting ourselves go"? It is true that women often lose touch with their bodies, but why is this?

Our society has a belief that to be a mother. You have to be selfless - translating into "less care for self than others," which often leads to "minimal or no care" for self. Families will take as much as mothers give, and it is very important for mothers to know their limits and make time for themselves.

We have not been taught to value the mother. Women have to work harder and harder to prove their value, not only as mothers and wives but in the workplace. And for women who have to juggle careers, parenting, marriage expectations, community involvement, taking care of their own aging parents, being sleep deprived... there is not a lot of time left in the day to tend to themselves – so they become disconnected from their own needs and often end up compromising their own health.

In order to keep ourselves from becoming "bitter" (pardon the expression), I encourage women to practice mindfulness in addition to physical and nutritional self-care. We need to feel that we are worthy of taking care of ourselves. We also really need to support each other, understand each other, defend rather than judge each other, cheer each other on, and find times to laugh with each other.

I think having a self-care journal is an excellent practice. We can keep track of things we do every day that benefit just us women (physical activity, time alone, taking a walk, a bath, reading a book, gardening, singing, any art outlet, prayer or meditation, learning a new skill, language or instrument. Connecting to Gratitude every day by keeping a Gratitude Journal is transformative and one of the things that I recommend for all my clients – especially women. Make the time – go within, find yourself, and tend to your own internal garden.

Claire Neilsen is the owner of Clarity Health and Wellness and Elixir for Life and a Marriage Commissioner.

...

Marcus Aurelius

"Everything we hear is an opinion, not a fact. Everything we see is a perspective, not the truth."

2

KIM MALLORY

CHANGE YOUR MINDSET, CHANGE YOUR LIFE

We are all on a journey. Are you enjoying yours? We have twenty-four hours a day, and if you spend more than 20% of your life doing something that doesn't float your boat, you could be doing yourself a major disservice. I use the 80/20 rule with everything because life isn't perfect, but it should be enjoyable. I'll do an internal check: "Am I happy at least 80% of the time in my relationships, work, and life balance?" This is a great starting point if you need help to determine if you need help! I'm going to guess that there is room for improvement for everyone!!

Since I decided that "life was too short," I've gone from an insecure young woman that thought she "couldn't" to a thriving entrepreneur living a life that gets me out of bed in the morning, excited for what's next. I have the freedom to make my own choices for work and pleasure, and I'm my own boss, and I have total and complete control creatively. Has it been easy? Nope. But it's been worth it. Every challenge I've faced has turned into an experience that has taught me valuable lessons or led me on a path that aligns more with my heart. Not only have I realized this for myself, but I've seen it occur for countless other women.

YOU are the creator of the life that you dream of, but change is ultimately up to *you*. Books, courses, and inspirational videos can help you get started, but taking action is the core of taking responsibility for the direction of your life, and sometimes that can be a bit scary. Okay. Who am I kidding? It's freaking terrifying!! Yet incredibly empowering!

Luckily, taking action isn't nearly as hard as you might think —because every change, big or small, happens just one step at a time for everyone. Instead, the most important part of your success is something under your complete control. Your MINDSET!

Mindset is defined as a set of beliefs or a way of thinking that determines one's actions, reactions, and attitudes. In other words, mindset is how we think and how those thoughts guide our decisions and actions. All of us have a mindset, whether we realize it or not. And that mindset can be either helpful or harmful.

A harmful mindset can keep us from reaching our full potential and achieving our goals. It can cause us to give up easily, miss out on opportunities, and make bad decisions. On the other hand, a helpful mindset can help us persevere through difficult times, take advantage of opportunities that come our way, and make good decisions.

Mindset matters because it colors everything. It shapes how we see things, interpret events, react to challenges, and interact with others. Mindset can be a powerful force for good, help us achieve our goals, overcome adversity, and find happiness and satisfaction in life. A negative mindset can do just the opposite. It can cause us to give up on our dreams, dwell on our failures and miss out on the joys of life. Mindset matters because it shapes everything about us - our thoughts, emotions, behavior, and even physical health.

A change in mindset changes how we see the world, how we interact with others, and how we feel about ourselves. It can be a life-changing experience. Let's choose a mindset that will lead us to a better life. Luckily, there are some things we can do to change our mindset for the better.

Three keys to changing your mindset:

- Adopt a Growth Mindset - become the person who believes they can improve their skills, prospects, and lives by learning new things
- Identify limiting beliefs
- Find like-minded supportive individuals

Blast through your limiting beliefs

Many limiting beliefs are subconscious habits that we don't even know are affecting us. Observing our automatic thoughts can be done in a number of ways.

Focus on your breathing and simply relax. Subconscious negative beliefs will often rise to the surface and attempt to disrupt the tranquility. Note them and write them down.

Free write about your dream goal—and what's keeping you from success. This is a great way to identify your limiting beliefs. Seeing them on paper often shows how silly some of your negative self-talk is. Ask yourself "why" as you write down the beliefs to drill down deep.

Ask a trusted friend for their honest assessment to help identify roadblocks as well as your strengths. Find someone who's non-judgmental and whose opinion you trust.

When you have a limiting belief that starts with I can't, I won't, I don't, I'm not. Start over and replace it with I can, I will, I am.

Why be Normal?

This has got to be the #1 most freeing thing that I ever let go of. If you can find it within you to do things without worrying about the opinions of others - You will thrive.

When I look back now at all of the comments or opinions that made me doubt myself or stay in a profession that wasn't working for me because of others' fears, it is mind-blowing. My life purpose became crystal clear when I decided I didn't care what other people might think.

When I allowed myself the freedom to be different, I made the decision to block out the chatter of those that were stuck in their lives or couldn't see past their pay cheques. I decided that was their problem, not mine, and suddenly, my decisions were no longer muddied by the unsolicited opinion of others or my own insecurities of "what will people think." Choose to live life. Choose to be creative. Choose to be multi-faceted.

Choose happiness. "normal" people will put their fears on you. You are not normal.

You are wild and passionate. Wild women are freedom seekers and care more about helping people and changing the world than they do about status. They choose happiness, and you can too.

Kim Mallory is a published author, Holistic Wellness Coach and Business Mentor.

.

...

Albert Schweitzer

"Sometimes our light goes out but is blown again into instant flame by an encounter with another human being."

3

BRENDA COOPER

"You are never too old to set another goal
or to dream a new dream."
C.S. Lewis

WHAT I KNOW TO BE TRUE

TRUE FRIENDSHIPS
Best friends you can count on just one hand
Look left, or right there they will stand
There are those who are just passing through
Then ones that deceive and wound you too
The tears I have shed for those untrue
Tear at my heart for what they could do
There are Friends that you hold so dear to your heart
When tragedy strikes it rips you apart
Your heart is so heavy with your daily cry
You can't comprehend why they had to die
Their voice is fading, their touch now is gone

But they're still in your dreams until it is dawn
Friendships are precious, I know this to be true
Those friends are forever beloved by you

ENTANGLED

Family blood is not always so kind
Some throw you into a toxic grind
How can someone just turn on a dime
Or did they spin this web with vengeance in mind
Betrayal and defeat are part of the pain
A severed bond is what has remained
I have walked away, as they were out of control
My broken heart is left to console
How did this ever come to be?
Once there were four, and now only three
Time has not been forgiving, not in this case
What was once held so dear is now a disgrace
Maybe one day it can all be healed
When the truth of it all can be revealed
My emotions are so heavy when I think of you
I am sorrowed by this, I know this to be true

HOLDING ON

Physical abuse or abuse of the mind
Can be overcome with support and time
The stigma that remains is not so forgiving
You must stand and fight and keep on living
The terror, the darkness of feeling alone
The fear of going back to what is unknown
The suffering, the torment that you have endured
The scars that were inflicted are now all obscured
The stolen innocence and trust that was once there

What has it left? It has stripped you bare
Don't stumble through life without seeking some peace
Look for that solace, you need that release
Don't be afraid to live deeply again
This is a new beginning and not the end
Let go of the past and all that you knew
Take back the control of what you've been through
The light is there, reach out, take hold
Hold someone's hand so you can be bold
The future is bright I know this to be true
I have walked these paths just like you

DON'T HESITATE
Take your wings and fly, fly high
Reach for your dreams, reach to the sky
Every step you take your heart beats stronger
Don't wait, don't hesitate, as it just takes longer
Life is not always what you want it to be
It's up to you to set yourself free
Hold tight to your dreams don't let them die
This you know well, and you can not deny
Dreams are your vision, your future they hold
Listen to their wisdom as your life will unfold
Dreams can be a reality, I know this to be true
As I am living my dream, and so can you

Lao Tzu

"Knowing others is intelligence; knowing yourself is true wisdom. Mastering others is strength; mastering yourself is true power."

4

SARAH MCLEAN

"Let go of who you think you're supposed to be;
embrace who you are."
Brene Brown

You are incredibly amazing. You have so much goodness inside of you and can achieve wondrous things. You can love, cry, laugh, and feel many incredible emotions.

You can be accepting, encouraging and supportive. You can be an advocate for what you believe in. You can be passionate. You can bring your dreams to life.

It's time to shake off the doubts and fears and start believing in yourself enough to take the first step. That first step is the most difficult, but it is the most powerful. It is the step that will lead you to amazing things if you let it. It is the step that will lead you to shine your own light, speak your own voice, and dance to your own song.

There are so many possibilities out there if only we are brave enough to believe in ourselves and see the potential of what we can achieve rather than thinking about the negatives of what we can't achieve.

It's time to own your power and take charge of your own life. It's time to love who you are and see how capable you are of achieving amazing things. It's time to energize yourself with what you love and then spread that love to your family, friends, and every corner of the world you can reach.

It's time to be brave enough to ditch the shackles of fear and judgment and allow yourself to follow the power of your heart.

...

Adrienne Rich

"There must be those among whom we can sit down and weep and still be counted as warriors."

5

MARY KOHL

"When one passes over, they are not truly gone!!"
Unknown

My parents died two weeks apart. I was young when it happened. I felt like I was all alone. Even though I was married with children, I felt alone.

It took about a year for me to sit down and tell my husband and children that I was sorry, as it was a rough year for me.

I started to talk about my parents, too, whoever would listen about all the beautiful things they taught me, and the way my father would say little quotes about life. I today say those quotes to everyone, and the more I spoke of them, it was like they were still here with us all.

If you stop talking about someone you love or care about when they pass over, that's when they are truly gone. It's okay to talk and tell stories about them, and remember it's okay to laugh, smile, or cry.

Remembering doesn't fill the loss. It helps ease the pain.

...

Lao Tzu

"When I let go of what I am, I become what I might be."

6

DANA L DEANE

"Don't cry when the sun is gone because
the tears won't let you see the stars."
Violeta Parra

Imagine a bright sunny day in early August.

The birds are chirping, and the trees are glistening with early morning dew. You are at the bottom of a beautiful ravine, a safe and wonderful place. Enveloped by Mother Nature. A bustle is going on around you as friends and family begin pouring in. Over the rise, you see a line of six men dressed in black forming an impenetrable force as they saunter down the ravine.

To your right is a man playing Amazing Grace on the bagpipes as the ravine fills with people. As you look up, two bald eagles are circling the community below with wings outstretched and offerings of Peace for those below.

Somewhere you can hear the faint tune of Stairway to Heaven...And you remember....

Today is THE day of your 25-year-old son's funeral. A day of celebration and being connected to the Divine Source. A day he would have you rejoice, not mourn. A day to remember all that he was and all he gave to this world—a sacred remembrance of his legacy.

It is in death that we welcome true connection, unity, honor, and love in all its forms. We are to be held with deep sentiment and devotion in both life and death.

...

Marissa Mayer

"I always did something I was a little not ready to do. I think that's how you grow. When there's that moment of Wow, I'm not really sure I can do this, and you push through those moments, that's when you have a breakthrough."

7

LYNDSEY SCOTT

"Appreciate and Value who truly Cares, Smile and Breathe
and let your Worries go,
So, Just Sip your Tea Nice and Slow."
Ann Lee Tzu Pheng

Tomorrow is never promised. This I know to be true…

A mother has many fears and worries when it comes to being a parent. Right from the moment, she becomes pregnant to the moment of giving birth and beyond. The fears never go away but change as our children grow.

As a mother of five, I can attest to this and the fact that those fears still come with every pregnancy. There are even fears I have that I have said, "Oh, that could never happen to me" let me tell you, it can.

On Saturday, June 4, 2022, at 3:03 am, I received a call that would change my life forever.

My firstborn had been in a fatal car accident. At that moment, my heart shattered, and I became a whirl of emotions that even I still can't fully understand today.

At 3:28 am, I watched as my son was being rolled out of the ambulance and through the Emergency doors. At that very moment, every emotion slipped away except one, RELIEF.

Relief that my son was alive.

As the days started to pass and the pieces came together, I was filled with emotions and questions that I couldn't understand or may never have answers to. Except for one thing for sure is true.

Tomorrow is never promised.

So, I ask you to hold your loved ones close and tell them how much you love them. Last but not least, tell your babies to call home. No matter the situation, ALWAYS call home.

...

Dalai Lama

"The purpose of our lives is to be happy."

8

DANA K. CARTWRIGHT

"Whatever satisfies the soul is truth."
Walt Whitman

What I know to be true is humans seek truth.

If you speak the truth, people begin to trust you. As they trust, they invite you to the door of their heart. If you continue to speak the truth, they cautiously open their heart.

As truth dominates, they welcome you to "see" their true self, which is always a treasure. A human can give no greater gift than the entrance to their heart.

In one's heart lies their truth, their magnificent gifts which never disappoint.

Thomas A. Edison

"Many of life's failures are people who did not realize how close they were to success when they gave up."

9

KATELIN STANVICK

"Success is not how high you have climbed,
but how you make a positive difference to the world."
Roy T. Bennett

Her inner child was wounded from a young girl around the age of four. Domestic violence and addictions are the leading cause of what destroyed my family.

From that moment forward, my trauma began leaving me with emotions that I never understood why I was feeling these.

As I am on my healing journey, these emotions still seem to get the best of me; However, now, I can work through these with healthy coping mechanisms and keep going with resiliency.

I was in survival mode, always wanting to fight everyone who came into my life. I never knew what it was like to have healthy coping mechanisms to build those healthy relationships. I became rebellious and thought I knew everything there was to know.

One day after I had my daughter and moved away from my hometown, I told myself that I had a choice to either get my shit together or I would lose my daughter. I never want her to face the life I did, so I decided to fight for what I believed in, which was myself, my health, and the desire to create the life I always dreamt of having. I put myself through upgrading and then through a four-year bachelor's degree. Remembering when I thought I knew it all, well, I knew very little about life.

My degree taught me much about myself and why I faced adversity throughout my adolescence and young adulthood. I believe those who practice healing, self-love, and peeling back those layers to heal the wounded inner child will become stronger.

I know I am where I am supposed to be at this moment; Nonetheless, through believing in yourself, strength, and resiliency, you can be too.

J.K. Rowling

"It is our choices that show what we truly are,
far more than our abilities."

10

WOODSIDE LISA

"To err is human."
Alexander Pope

One thing I know for sure is that we, as humans, are like alphabet soup. I find people fascinating because we all have LETTERS.

Our letters don't define us but rather pre-dispose us to have certain traits, skills, handicaps, and emotional highs and lows.

Some really super people I know battle ADD, ADHD, OCD, PTSD, ADDM, ASD, BD, BPD, CD, DMDD, FAS ID, LD, and this list goes on.

What are your letters and how well do you know you? How well do you know, understand, and appreciate those super people in your life?

In my fifties, I've just only really acknowledged and appreciated my letters. I know and understand who I really am and what makes me me. Sometimes salty, sometimes sweet, and always interrupting.

Every person is different and unique. Be true to you.

Life is a rollercoaster, isn't it? Luckily there are joyful and comedic events (I consider yay days) to get us through the tragic events, mishaps, and missteps in life.

We are all imperfectly perfect with a mish-mash of letters, but this is what makes getting to know you, women like me, a fascinating experience.

...

Drew Barrymore

"Life is very interesting… in the end, some of your greatest pains, become your greatest strengths."

11

CHRISTINE LUCIANI

"Courage, dear heart."
C.S. Lewis

I have always thought I could not be happy on my own, that I would be too lonely, that I would not be able to stand it. As I have aged, I have discovered this is not true. The truth is we are all capable of being happy on our own.

We all need socialization with friends and family, of course, but I am not defined by whether or not I am alone.

The world seems to expect that we all should be couples, that we all should have a significant other. I disagree.

Celebrate yourself, live and love the way you want, and have the courage to be yourself... all the time. I am not saying everyone should be alone. That would be silly. I am saying that we are all stronger than we think... be happy with yourself, and a whole new world of possibilities opens.

It is easier than you think, and that is the truth.

...

Anne Frank

"Parents can only give good advice or put them on the right paths, but the final forming of a person's character lies in their own hands."

12

TRISH SCOULAR

"Only one thing is more frightening than speaking your truth,
and that is not speaking."
Naomi Wolf

My truth has been secured in my ability to find my voice and to speak my truth, which has led me towards loving myself.

Most of my life, I have been worried about what others think of me, causing me to remain silent and feeling bad as a result. Thinking to myself, if only I had said this or responded like that, oh next time I will; the next time arrives, and the story is stuck on repeat leaving a cycle hard to step out of.

Why is it so hard to let the words roll out of our mouths, liberating us in our truth, standing up to our core of what we value and the worth we know we are? This inability is what creates those core and limiting beliefs that are hard to shake.

A passive-aggressive tone that is not the assertive note we need to allow our authentic self and worthiness to surface and our confidence to shine. When we become clear in our values, we will notice a shift. When we begin to say it is not okay for you to disrespect me or to put me down, we begin to feel alive.

It is a comfort zone that shows discomfort, and the more we lean into becomes easier with each step. The bloom blossoms, and the truth of how we feel changes in the way we carry ourselves, allowing us to become healthier in our response and our choices.

...

Brigham Young

"You educate a man; you educate a man.
You educate a woman; you educate a generation."

13

SHERON CHISHOLM

"A conviction that you are a daughter of God gives you a feeling of comfort in your self-worth. It means that you can find strength in the balm of Christ. It will help you meet the heartaches and challenges with faith and serenity."
James E. Faust

I know for certain that I am a daughter of the King. That makes me a Princess and a sister in Christ. There is nothing that I do that can change this because the Love of God is in me and guides me in the direction he wants me to go.

I know that I make mistakes, and I am forgiven by his grace and mercy. His presence in my life gives me the strength to do the things I do, and without it, I know I would never have been able to raise three special needs children on my own or anything else I've accomplished.

The greatest and most important thing I gave to my children was that Jesus loves everyone, and we have the responsibility to spread God's Love to everyone by what we do and say.

Although I tried to be a good role model for my children, I was not totally successful, and I trust that the seed is planted, and God will take it from there.

What I know for sure is that God loves everyone, and he wants us to go out into the world and plant seeds of his love so that he can bring them into his kingdom.

What a joy that gives me, and that's what keeps me going. If we want more joy in the world, we have to go out there and give it away. I know for sure that I have the Joy of the Lord in my heart, and I want it to tell everyone that Jesus loves them.

...

Jane Austen

"It isn't what we say or think that defines us,
but what we do."

14

MICHELLE VOYAGEUR

"You will face many defeats in life,
But never let yourself be defeated."
Maya Angelou

There are many lessons I have learned along the path of life. Some were invaluable, and most were crucial. I base these valuable tidbits on what my mom has shown me.

I am the second eldest in a family with five siblings. One of my truths came from this living situation. I was given much responsibility and knew that my younger brothers and sister looked to me for guidance and support. While I made many mistakes growing up, I was always caring and truthful with my siblings. I ensured that they knew that telling a lie would be something they would regret later. And when caught in a lie, there would be consequences. Truthfulness was the only way.

My mother also taught me about unconditional love. I knew this and grew this with my own daughters. They, in turn, have done the same with their own children. I have three amazing, strong, beautiful daughters with whom I am very close.

In fact, I now live with two of them and two of my grandchildren, and let's not forget my son-in-law. I feel like this would not be possible if not for the close bond that we share. They know I have made sacrifices for them and would do just about anything for them. I feel in my heart that having this unconditional love is my strongest truth. We have no secrets and know everything about each other.

These are the things I know to be true.

When I felt defeated along the way, I knew I simply had to ask for help from my daughters, and they would rally around me and help me get back up.

...

Bernhard Berenson

"Miracles happen to those who believe in them."

15

LINDA S NELSON

"Change will not come if we wait for some other person or some other time. We are the ones we've been waiting for. We are the change that we seek."
Barak Obama

The question – what do I know to be true for this book – was posed at a time when yet another school shooting took place in an elementary school in my beloved country. And my broken heart for all those impacted made me ask lots of questions.

What has happened to the world I live in? How did we get here? Why does this keep happening? How are we raising our children to think so little of life and how precious and sacred it is? What can we do to change our world so we don't have to experience this deep pain as a country again?

I thought the words would come easily to the original question – what do I know to be true?

After all, I've lived on this planet now for 71 years – and counting. And maybe – because I've lived a while – I often DO take time to reflect back and view my life and the world I live in with a different perspective.

I'm able to see the history of other troubled times in our past – and how we've solved them to make the world a better place. But I seemed to be asking more questions – than answering the question before me. What do I know to be true? After much thought and reflection, I settled on this truth.

We are the change we want to see in the world. It starts with us. It is easy to look around and find reasons for why bad things happen in the world – and blame events, circumstances, and people for the problems we face.

But I know this to be true. One person changes the world – one positive encounter at a time. We need to look within first. If we want to change things, we must first change ourselves. That's where the answers lie – that's where the power lies.

We were created to make a difference in this world. And we have a choice in how we're going to do it. We're all given special gifts that are meant to be used for the benefit of others. We all have the privilege and the responsibility to others to use these gifts we have. We all have been given a circle of influence – it could be our family, our friends, an organization, our work – wherever we encounter others.

How will YOU impact the world? You have the power to decide. Start with you. And change will happen one person at a time for the better.

...

Michelle Obama

"If you tap into your true story and share that truth, it will resonate with people."

16

PAULINE AWINO ATITWA

"Keep your face to the sunshine,
and you cannot see a shadow."
Helen Keller

I know God and want to say what I know is true about him. God is spirit. If you want anything, have faith in God, and your needs will be met.

When I read the Bible about the women of faith, my heart sings, and I am happy.

Women are the givers. Sister Dorcas, in the Bible, was a good helper for widows and prepared the altar of God right up until the time she died.

The servants of God prayed for her to return to life again because they loved her so much.

When you love God, and you love and care for widows and the children living in orphanages, you are giving back to God in a fantastic way. And God will then give back to you.

This is true of what I know and love.

God bless you all, and amen. Acts 9:36

Deep Roy

"Inspiration comes from within yourself. One has to be positive. When you're positive, good things happen."

17

COLINDA LAVIOLETTE

"Whatever the present moment contains,
accept it as if you had chosen it."
Eckhart Tolle

What I know to be true... within my personal life experience is that God/Creator/Universe does not discriminate between good/bad, negative/positive, joyfulness/heaviness.

I've come to learn and witness firsthand what I am focused most strongly on, what I expect and look for in life. What I feel strongest emotionally, even those things that I don't speak of, are what I experience and see in life.

When I am in a space of balance, of "flow/alignment with life and all creation," all is well within my world, everything seems to fall into place with synchronicity. Needs are met, the right people at the right time are encountered, and things seem just to come together perfectly and out of the blue when we need them.

Likewise, when in a state of heaviness. Then, nothing seems to go well; everything that possibly could seems to go sideways. Reminding myself in these circumstances that they are temporary, a return to balance is always attainable.

Following a daily spiritual practice, understanding that surrender is a process, not just an instant letting go and utilizing the process to release what I need to instead of trying to be in control of all my circumstances and experiences.

Being compassionate with self when things are difficult, finding the lessons, teachings, and blessings in all situations, good or bad. Daily self-care in ways that are suitable for me to keep balance, having faith, and trusting that the Universe always has my back. Following and understanding natural/ancestral law have all been key for myself in this experience we call life.

...

Les Brown

"In every day, there are 1,440 minutes.
That means we have 1,440 daily opportunities
to make a positive impact."

18

HEATHER SCOTT

"With every experience, you alone are painting your own canvas, thought by thought, choice by choice."
Oprah Winfrey

What I know to be true is that everything in life is a choice. "Good Bad or Indifferent ."The choices you make influence who you become…

If someone hurts you and you stay in your anger, it is no longer their issue. It is yours. You have made a choice to stay in the anger and not to move on. You cannot control the behavior of others; you can, on the other hand, make a choice on how you handle your response.

You can't change the fact that bad things are going to happen in your life. Having said that, you have the choice to learn from the experience and grow.

Decision-making is a process of making choices by identifying a decision, gathering information, and weighing the pros and cons of how that choice is going to affect us in the future. I also know it to be true that your "Gut Instinct and Intuition" plays a big part in the choices we make. It is okay to listen to your gut instinct/intuition.

I wasn't looking for a job when a job came looking for me. Someone made a choice to give my name to someone who was looking for a manager for one of their insurance offices. When they contacted me, I made a choice to go to the interview because I thought that if I didn't, I would always wonder. Nearly 13 years later, I know that I made the right choice by weighing the benefits the company had to offer. It was a no-brainer.

As you move through life with the Good, Bad, or Indifferent situations and people that touch your life, it is your choice who moves forward in your journey with you...Choose Wisely!

...

Michelle Obama

"Find people who will make you better."

19

SABRINA LAMBERT

"Your reality is as you perceive it to be. So, it is true
that by altering our perception, we can alter our reality."
William Constantine

When you have been divorced once, the experience acts like
a warning system to prevent similar mistakes. Not planning
to marry again, I still chose to marry my best friend, and we
were blessed with a precious daughter a year later. Our lives
involved work and home life, raising our daughter.

When she was a teenager, I noticed our marriage felt
different. Spending so much time as mom and dad, we had
lost our spark. No disagreements, no hurtful words, yet those
loving courtesies that energize a relationship were absent too.
Warning signals, should I be ready for another split?

Our daughter still needed both of us. Could our lost intimacy
be found?

While on vacation, watching the sunset on the Pacific Ocean together as a family, I knew I was not ready to give up. Spurred on to discover the couple we could become, I suspected the harsh truth, that maybe, it was me. After all, I was the one feeling badly about how we interacted. Maybe I needed to change the way I was feeling and showing up as a partner.

Starting slow, as an experiment, I chose kind and loving responses instead of a matter-of-fact reply. I did simple, meaningful tasks like making morning coffee for my partner. Behaving as someone who demonstrates love and care for their partner, I suddenly felt happier. And it rubbed off on my husband too.

My experiment proved what I now know to be true. Love is a choice.

Lao Tzu

"In the end, the treasure of life is missed by those
who hold on and gained by those who let go."

20

SUSAN DABORN

"What goes around comes around."
Unknown

What I know to be true is that asking for help is not a weakness but just the opposite - it takes courage to reach out.

Asking for help actually empowers you, so don't be afraid to ask or receive it.

Along with that, being able to say NO without guilt or feeling bad is so important. By saying NO, it doesn't mean you have to explain why or justify it in any way.

For me, it has taken half my life to learn to say no, ask for help and feel good about it. For me, it was very freeing to get to that point, and it has made such a difference in my healing and life.

...

Libba Bray

"You can never know about your own destiny. Are the people you meet there to play a part in your own destiny, or do you exist just to play a role in theirs?"

21

SHANNON LEVEE

"Nothing ever goes away until it has taught us
what we need to know."
Pema Chodron

What I know to be true is that "nothing ever goes away until it has taught us what we need to know." This quote slapped me across the face the other day as I realized I let them away with it again.

So much for saying, I have figured out how to set "Healthy Boundaries" because that would be a crock of dodo. However, I am much better than I was eight years ago... yay me, and more yay to my team of therapists, cheerleaders, spiritual mentors, and recovery family.

You know that one loved one that keeps coming back to take from you, take advantage of you or suck the life out of you? They will continue to show up on your doorstep with their hands out.... UNTIL YOU SAY "NO" and stick to it. Or, to make it a bit easier on you, educate yourself on how to make "agreements."

Boundaries seem too harsh for some of us but making an agreement is much softer. It's a two-way conversation with some wiggle room. My loved one is not going away, and I don't want them to, but I do appreciate the new earned respect we have for each other since we established our agreements.... most of the time.

...

Deepak Chopra

"Each of us is a unique strand in the intricate web of life
and here to make a contribution."

22

KAREN COLEMAN

"It's all about the love."
Unknown

Things I know to be true

Well, hi, everyone. I've had dogs all my life, and I want to share an incredible story of my incredible dog named Sammy, who was so special.

This dog I rescued from a shelter was half Chow and half Labrador, and he looks like a hundred-pound black bear! He had the Chow tongue, which meant it was black. And he had a black coat with a huge chest… he was gorgeous.

He was well trained and was like a nine-year-old little boy; he was very protective of me and only liked me and my son. We were his pack, and he took his job very seriously. His bark was that of a lion.

Now big dogs only live to be about ten, eleven, or twelve, but he lived to be two months shy of his 17th birthday. My vet told me, "He loves you so much, Karen. He just doesn't want to leave you."

But one morning, when he was almost 17 years old, he got up at 4:30 in the morning and fell into my closet! It startled me, and I woke up. When I looked into his eyes, his eyes were flashing back and forth, and he could not maintain a gaze. He couldn't even stand up. I knew from my nursing that he suffered a brain injury and had a stroke.

I handled the emergency very well since my training had just kicked in. He couldn't walk. I tried to pick him up, but I couldn't. He couldn't go outside; he couldn't do anything. So, I called my vet at 4:30 in the morning and told him what was happening. I feel so blessed that my vet said to me, "I'll meet you at the office in 20 minutes."

I managed with a sheet to pick up my dog, my blessed sweet old man of a dog. I put him in my truck and drove as fast as possible to my vet because I didn't want him to suffer. The vet's clinic didn't open until 9:00 am.

The vet helped me get Sammy out of my truck when I arrived at the clinic. We cradled him in the sheet and brought him to the back entrance of the vet's clinic. We laid him gently on the floor. My vet took one look at him, and he said, "Karen, if you have anything you want to say to him, say it now because once I get the IV started in him and give him the medication, he will go really fast."

So, I did. As I cradled him and whispered the last words he heard in his ears, and I nodded to my vet. My vet injected the medication, and he just fell asleep in my arms. I cried like a baby all the way home.

Of all the dogs I've had, he was the only one that I had cremated, and he sits on my dresser in our bedroom. Every once in a while, I shake his little urn up and talk to him. I'll always have him with me.

It took me many years to get over his loss, and even thinking about getting another dog is hard.

You know it's coming, you're never prepared for it, but this I know for sure to be true… I loved him unconditionally, and he loved me…unconditionally.

...

Richard Matheson

"All of us have a path to follow and the path begins on earth."

23

SAMANTHA TRARBACK

"The hardest thing in this world is to live in it."
Buffy the Vampire Slayer

What I know to be true is that people are the only creatures that live based on choice and not instinct. I and I alone are in control of how I feel and react to things.

I know my heart beats outside of me and radiates to my daughter. Watching her and seeing her grow makes me want to be a better person, to be the person she says I am.

I am a work in progress. Changing my mind, ideas, and views doesn't make me a hypocrite. It shows I can listen and grow. I am not ashamed of the person I was. The young woman who thought she knew it all and was surrounded by toxic people. I decided to be around them and follow their views.

As I grew up and grew more confident, I was able to be secure in my beliefs and views. I realized my personal values and understood that change was good. It was scary, but it was good. It meant I was growing.

I know these are things that I want to teach my daughter. To be confident and strong. To have her voice so she can say no and demand respect. What I know to be true is while everything is always changing, I can be assured my faith and love for my family is always growing.

...

Shannon L. Alder

"The true definition of mental illness is when the majority of
your time is spent in the past or future,
but rarely living in the realism of NOW."

24

IRENE SUTHERLAND

"As I stand in my power, I am aware at all times
when and where I choose to use it." Irene Sutherland

I am remembering who I am

I am One.

I am a woman who stands in wonder.

Who am I?

I am the bear who protects her young.

I am the butterfly in soft transformation.

I am the song on the lips of my tribe.

I am the earth; I am the sky.

I need not ask who I am. I will just be glad to be alive.

Therefore, I Am!

...

Hayley Williams

"Sometimes it takes a good fall to
really know where you stand."

25

JULIE BREAKS

"Change your thoughts, and you change your world."
Norman Vincent Peale

The quote above says exactly what I know to be true. We can have a better life, and it is within myself, not the outside world.

If I'm living as a victim of circumstance or living a life where I blame everyone for how my life has gone. That mindset will do me no good and only hold me back from the bright future I have waiting for me.

We think around 60 to 70 thousand thoughts per day, and the scary thing is that most are repeated thoughts of all those thoughts. And I found I was doing it every single day.

The day I understood that I was in control of my thoughts was when I went to work to change my way of thinking and my mindset. It didn't happen overnight; changing your thoughts takes quite some time. But by working on it daily, my thoughts become more positive daily.

Today, I can recognize when my mindset is moving towards the negative quite quickly. This awareness allows me to correct myself and change my thoughts so that I don't spiral into the victim or blaming mode.

It's true; if you change your thoughts, you change your life.

...

Suzanne Weyn

"Your life is an occasion. Rise to it."

26

TAM LISLLY

"Don't worry if people think you're crazy. You are crazy.
You have that kind of intoxicating insanity that lets other
people dream outside of the lines and become who
they're destined to be."
Jennifer Elisabeth

I've felt most of my life has been fighting people who want
me to change into something or someone I didn't want to be.

My parents put a lot of pressure on me when I was young.
They took me to dance, music lessons, enrolled me in sports
and had me in the best schools. I appreciated and loved my
parents for only wanting the best out of life for me. But what
they wanted for me was not what I wanted for myself.

My parents dreamed of me following in dad's footsteps and
becoming a doctor. However, this was not my dream.

My marriage fell apart because I didn't want to conform to the person my husband wanted me to be. It's not his fault. I know I didn't show him my true self because I was trying to be who he wanted me to be. I found that I could only pretend for so long.

Once I became aware that most of my life, I was someone I wasn't, I went on a clearing out of friends and family who didn't support me in my path to be my true self.

I stopped hiding the real me. I spoke with my parents about conforming to what everyone else wanted me to be. And the most astonishing thing happened. They understood and now support me in being the real me, with my goals and dreams for my life.

Now that I have stopped hiding, the people who genuinely love and support me have shown up in my life.

...

Marcus Aurelius

"Dwell on the beauty of life. Watch the stars and see yourself running with them."

27

ANNABELLE GOSEUM

"Every day may not be good…
but there's something good in every day."
Alice Morse Earle

I have faith. Not in the same way my parents or especially my grandparents had. They attended church every Sunday, and the church was a part of their daily lives. It was the place they not only went to worship but where they also went for their social life.

I remember going to church for many years with my family. And I enjoyed it. I loved listening to the sermons and couldn't wait for the after church potlucks.

Then in my early thirties, my beloved grandmother passed away. I had just returned home from her funeral and attended my church for the Sunday sermon. As I sat with the rest of the congregation, listening to our Pastor speaking, my mind was wandering, and I thought of my grandmother.

Then the Pastor said something that made my mind come back into the room. The Pastor was speaking about what happens when we die. He said that when someone dies, they stay asleep, waiting for the second coming of Jesus. When Jesus comes, he will raise the dead and take them to heaven.

I felt a wave of shivers from the top of my head to my feet. It was as though I had just woken up. Something told me this was not correct. For the first time in my life, I questioned what I heard. Although this was the teaching of my church, I had never before questioned this belief or any of the church's beliefs.

This was when my spiritual journey began. I stopped going to church. I believe in a higher power, and I pray and meditate daily. But I do it my way, with my truth as I believe it to be.

...

J.D. Stroube

"Life is filled with unanswered questions, but it is the courage to seek those answers that continues to give meaning to life. You can spend your life wallowing in despair, wondering why you were the one who was led towards the road strewn with pain, or you can be grateful that you are strong enough to survive it."

PART 2

———

LEARN MORE ABOUT WOMEN LIKE ME

28

THANK YOU TO THE WLM COMMUNITY

To our beautiful community members, thank you again for your support. For supporting the women like me community. For participating in our community books and for your encouragement and inspiration that flows from your hearts.

What you know to be true was a topic which was voted on by our members. This was an important topic that the members wanted to write about. And I'm so glad this topic was chosen.

As I read through all the submissions for the book, I found that everyone has their own truth. I love this. It shows how diverse we are as a society. Some truths are similar, but no truth was precisely the same. And isn't that how our world is to be?

And, as with our other books written by all of you, the proceeds go to charity. The proceeds will go to Breast Cancer Research. Thank you, ladies, for helping us with this very important cause.

With much appreciation and love,

Julie

...

Socrates

"The secret of change is to focus all of your energy
not on fighting the old, but on building the new."

29

JOIN THE WOMEN LIKE ME COMMUNITY

If you do not belong to **Women Like Me Community – Julie Fairhurst,** I would be pleased if you decided to join us.

The Women Like Me Community – Julie Fairhurst is a Facebook group of like-minded women. Women who want to pay it forward and lift others up and promote healing in the world. Ages range from 17 to 83 years of age from all over the world and from all walks of life.

As a community, we write community books, with the proceeds going to charity. Maybe you will join in on the next book?

Together, as a group, we can help promote healing in our world.

...

Mahatma Gandhi

"You must be the change your wish to see in the world."

30

MEET JULIE FAIRHURST

I'm Julie Fairhurst, the Founder of Women Like Me and Story Coach. I want to share with you how Women Like Me came into existence.

When I was ten years old, my mom killed her best friend in a car accident while driving drunk. Three little girls lost their mom that night. And so did I. My mom didn't physically die. She died inside and was never the same again.

Her life spiraled down due to shame and unbelievable guilt, and she took her children with her.

Drug addiction and alcoholism became rapid in my family. My siblings and myself were thrown into a life of chaos. It was entirely out of control.

I became pregnant at 14 years of age, married at 17, divorced at 29, and a single mother with three young children and a grade eight education. I thought my life was set for failure, following down my parents' path. I was headed in the wrong direction.

But, somewhere deep inside, that young girl inside showed up and reminded me that I wanted better for my life and the life of my children. I had no support from anyone, not a soul. I had to do it all on my own.

Was it an easy road? No, it was far from easy. I was a single mom for 24 years. We lived off government handouts. I stood in line at food banks to feed my kids. At Christmas, we received Christmas hampers, and I would go to the toy bank to get presents for the kids. The path we were on was not easy to change, especially when it was all you knew.

But I did it. I went back to school and finished my education. I built an outstanding career in sales, marketing and promotion. I won the company's top awards and was the first woman to achieve top salespeople year after year in a male-dominated industry. I was able to buy a home on my own and provide a stable environment to raise my children.

Some people say never to look back, but I do every day. Why? Because I never want to forget the journey that led me to where I am today. And today, my life is entirely different. I didn't just fall into this life. I worked at it every day, all the time.

Then, in 2019, my beautiful 24-year-old niece died from a drug overdose on the streets of Vancouver, Canada. And that was the day I said enough! My niece's death indirectly resulted from my mother's actions or non-actions and my siblings continuing with their destructive lifestyles.

When we don't deal with our traumas, we pass the dysfunction along to the next generation and the next. This is where my passion comes from, the reason I started Women Like Me. But I am only one person.

Now I am reaching out to you, you who would be in service of others, healers, coaches, and anyone who deals with the public personally. If you work with the public, you may not think you can help them change their lives, but you can.

I have started a movement, but I can't do it alone. It's time to share your stories with others to inspire change in their lives and help us all along our way.

Wayne Gretzky

"You miss 100 percent of the shots you never take."

31

IS IT TIME FOR YOU TO BECOME A PUBLISHED AUTHOR?

The **Women Like Me Academy** was formed to help you get your story out of your heart and head and into a book. Writing an entire book is a daunting task, and it can be so overwhelming that many of us will put writing on the back burner. And most times, it never gets written.

Writing a chapter of your story is a fantastic way to get your story out to the public, where it can be read and inspire others to make changes in their lives. Your chapter story can benefit you in many powerful ways. Let's talk about your story!

Is it time for you to become a published author?

Deciding which story of your life to write can be a confusing and daunting task. This alone has stopped many a writer. Not to worry! I excel at helping you draw your story from your head and heart and get it onto paper.

Together we can choose which of your life stories is the perfect one to use for the Academy. We will have a private conversation to flush out your story, so you feel comfortable opening up about what you think is the story you want to tell —the story which will benefit you in your life and help others.

Whether you are or are not a professional writer has nothing to do with you writing your story!

I will guide you every step of the way; if you are stuck, we will get you unstuck. Don't worry. I will keep you flowing. There will be editing of your chapter to ensure spelling, punctuation, and grammar are correct. You can do this; I know you can!

Becoming a published author gives you many tools to use to promote yourself and your story!

By the time we finish our time together, you will be ready to share your story with the world. And most importantly, you will gain the distinction of being called a Published Author.

If you want to learn more about the Academy, you can go here…

https://womenlikemestories.com/women-like-me-academy

Albert Einstein

"Strive not to be a success, but rather to be of value."

32

CONNECT WITH ME
WOULD YOU LIKE TO CONNECT WITH ME?

If you would like to reach out to me for any reason, I would love to connect with you. Here's how you can find me.

- julie@changeyourpath.ca
- www.womenlikemestories.com

Follow me on social media:

Facebook: Rock Star Strategies:

www.facebook.com/juliefairhurstcoaching

Instagram:Inspire by Julie:

https://www.instagram.com/womenlikemestories/

LinkedIn:

https://www.linkedin.com/in/womenlikemestories/

...

Mark Twain

"Twenty years from now you will be more disappointed by the things that you didn't do than by the ones you did do."

33

CONFIDENCE JOURNAL

If you would like to start a journal, please accept this gift from me. This is my free Confidence Journal. Here you will find links to some of my favorite motivational videos and other valuable tools to help you in your journey of discovery.

Link to the Free Confidence Journal
https://womenlikemestories.com/confidence-journal-free/

Harriet Tubman

"Every great dream begins with a dreamer. Always remember, you have within you the strength, the patience, and the passion to reach for the stars to change the world."

OTHER BOOKS BY JULIE FAIRHURST

Julie's books can be found on Amazon or on the
womenlikemestories.com website:

- Women Like Me Community - Messages To My
  Younger Self
- Women Like Me Community - Sharing Words Of
  Gratitude
- Self Esteem Confidence Journal Build Your Self
  Esteem - 100 Tips designed to boost your confidence
- Women Like Me - A Celebration of Courage and
  Triumphs (volume one)
- Women Like Me - Stories of Resilience and Courage
  (volume two)
- Women Like Me – A Tribute to the Brave and Wise
  (volume three)
- Women Like Me – Breaking Through The Silence
  (volume four)
- Positivity Makes All The Difference - Your Mindset
  Matters
- Agent Etiquette - 14 Things You Didn't Learn in
  Real Estate School
- 7 Keys to Success - How to Become a Real Estate
  Sales Badass
- 30 Days To Real Estate Action
- Net Marketing
- 100 Reasons Agents Quit

...

H. Jackson Brown, Jr.

"Remember that the happiest people are not those getting more, but those giving more."